Collins

Easy Learning

Grammar and punctuation practice

Age 7-9

My name is _____.

I am _____ years old.

I go to _____ School.

How to use this book

- Find a quiet, comfortable place to work, away from other distractions.
- Tackle one topic at a time.
- Help with reading the instructions where necessary and ensure your child understands what to do.
- Encourage your child to check their own answers as they complete each activity.
- Discuss with your child what they have learnt.
- Let your child return to their favourite pages once they have been completed, to talk about the activities.
- Reward your child with plenty of praise and encouragement.

Special features

- Yellow boxes: Introduce a topic and outline the key grammar or punctuation ideas.
- Red boxes: Emphasise a rule relating to the unit.
- Yellow shaded boxes: Offer advice to parents on how to consolidate your child's understanding.

Published by Collins
An imprint of HarperCollins*Publishers*
77–85 Fulham Palace Road
Hammersmith
London
W6 8JB

Browse the complete Collins catalogue at
www.collins.co.uk

© HarperCollins*Publishers* 2012

10 9 8 7 6 5 4 3 2

ISBN-13 978-0-00-746735-8

British Library Cataloguing in Publication Data

A Catalogue record for this publication is available from the British Library

Page design by G Brasnett, Cambridge
Illustrated by Kathy Baxendale, Steve Evans and Rachel Annie Bridgen
Cover design by Linda Miles, Lodestone Publishing
Cover illustration by Kathy Baxendale
Commissioned by Tammy Poggo
Project managed by Chantal Peacock
Printed in China

MIX
Paper from
responsible sources
FSC™ C007454

FSC™ is a non-profit international organisation established to promote the responsible management of the world's forests. Products carrying the FSC label are independently certified to assure consumers that they come from forests that are managed to meet the social, economic and ecological needs of present and future generations, and other controlled sources.

Find out more about HarperCollins and the environment at
www.harpercollins.co.uk/green

Contents

Sentences

Q1 Choose a beginning and an ending from the two lists to make complete sentences. Copy the complete sentences you have made.

We lay on the beach   sand in them.

The sea was   reading our books.

Our sandwiches had   cold but we had fun.

_____

_____

_____

Q2 Add the missing punctuation to the sentences.

Watch out, that dog looks cross_____   Come towards me slowly_____

Whose dog is it_____   The dog wandered off towards the pond_____

Q3 Write a sentence ending with:

a full stop

_____

a question mark

_____

an exclamation mark

_____

Give your child a sentence with the words jumbled up. Ask them to untangle the words so the sentence makes sense.

Nouns

Nouns are naming words.
Proper nouns are **nouns** that are the particular <u>name</u> of something, like a person, a day, a month, a special time or a place.

<u>T</u>illy went to <u>L</u>ondon on <u>S</u>aturday by train.

Proper nouns begin with capital letters.

Q1 Complete these sentences with a noun.

Every Monday I go to _____.

I enjoy reading my _____.

I saw a horse in a _____.

This morning I ate my _____.

Q2 Underline all the nouns in the sentences.

The horse cantered towards the hedge.

On Friday we are going to Cheltenham to visit Uncle Matt.

The dentist pulled out my wobbly tooth.

Q3 Answer these questions with a proper noun.

Which month comes before October? _____

What is the capital of Great Britain? _____

Who lives in Buckingham Palace? _____

What do many people celebrate during December? _____

What is the name of a famous footballer? _____

Ask your child to think of more questions like those found in **Q3** to ask other people. Remind your child that they need to be aware of the correct answers. All the answers should be proper nouns.

Verbs

A **verb** is usually a doing word.

It tells us what is happening (present tense) or what has already happened (past tense).

Tyler **kicks** the ball.
(**present tense**)

Tyler **kicked** the ball.
(**past tense**)

Q1 Complete the sentences with a verb from the box.

> **bought**   **broke**   **licks**   **sat**   **mows**

Dan _____ his ice cream quickly.

Dad _____ the lawn every Saturday.

Sarah _____ a newspaper at lunchtime.

The swing _____ when Jay _____ on it.

Q2 Complete the table with the verbs.

drank   *wrote*

painted

Present tense verbs	Past tense verbs

sleeps   *skips*

laughs

danced   *shouts*

Q3 Write two of your own sentences in the past tense.
(Past tense = something that has already happened)

_____

_____

Mime some actions and ask your child to write the 'action' word you are miming. Then ask him/her to write the verb in the past tense. This might highlight the fact that verbs can be regular (smile, smiled) or irregular (sing, sang).

Adjectives 1

Adjectives are describing words.
They tell us more about **nouns**.

> The hen laid **brown** eggs.
> The hen laid **big** eggs.
> The hen laid **two** eggs.

Q1 Circle the adjective in each sentence.

The Walton family walked in the cold wind.

The toddler slipped on the wet mud.

The three children ran to the park.

The grumpy cat scratched Tom's hand.

Q2 Complete each sentence with an adjective.

Mum made a _____ lunch.

The _____ dog had fun on the beach.

The _____ sun rose high in the sky.

Hannah forgot her _____ coat.

Q3 Write these adjectives into your own sentences.

lumpy _____

cold _____

loud _____

funny _____

It helps children if they realise there are different categories of adjectives, e.g. colour adjectives, number adjectives, number-order adjectives (e.g. third), comparative and superlative adjectives (see p. 26).

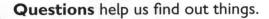

Questions

A **question** begins with a **capital letter** and ends with a **question mark**.

What shall we do today?

Questions help us find out things.

Q1 Write three questions you would like to ask an adult. Write down who you are going to ask. (Hint: It might be your teacher, the Queen, your aunty or dad.)

Who my questions are for: _____

My questions: _____

_____

_____

Q2 Write a question for each of these answers.

I'm going to take my coat.

_____

We are going to a restaurant.

_____

Yes, I'll buy some milk on the way home.

_____

We will arrive in the morning at about 11am.

_____

Discuss different types of questions with your child. Closed questions can be answered with a 'yes' or 'no'. Open questions have a variety of different answers. Think of a famous person and ask your child to ask closed questions to discover who it might be.

Exclamations

This is an **exclamation mark** !
It can be used at the end of a **sentence** to show *shock, fear, pain, danger, humour, surprise, joy, anger* or *an order*.

I love it!

Q1 Complete the table with the exclamations.
Remember to add the exclamation marks.

Don't touch

Quick, get over here

Watch out

That hurt

Ouch, please don't

Pain!	Surprise!	An order!

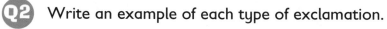

Help, I can't move my foot

I don't believe it

Stop, right now

Wow, look at that

Q2 Write an example of each type of exclamation.

shock _____

anger _____

upset _____

joy _____

Show your child different facial expressions, then ask them to write an exclamation that might go with each one.

Nouns can be **singular** or **plural**.
Singular means *one*.
Plural means *more than one*.

You add **s** to many singular nouns to make them plural.
If the singular noun ends in *sh*, *ch*, *ss* or *x* you add **es** to make the noun plural.

church ⟶ church**es**   kiss ⟶ kiss**es**

Q1 Complete the table.

Singular	Plural
class	
	foxes
dish	
	glasses
lunch	
	bushes

Q2 Underline the plural nouns in the sentences.

The dresses looked beautiful on the bridesmaids.

The apples and peaches tasted delicious.

The farmer checked his fields before letting in the cows.

Mrs Damage dropped the tray of dishes and glasses.

Q3 Write the plural nouns you have underlined in **Q2** in their singular form.

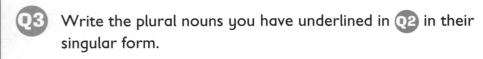

_____   _____   _____

_____   _____   _____

Articles (a and an)

It is important to know if **a** or **an** is needed in front of a word.
a is used in front of words beginning with a consonant.

a dog   **a** monkey

an is usually used in front of words beginning with a vowel.
The letters **a e i o u** are vowel letters.

an orange   **an** elephant

Q1 Add **a** or **an** in front of these nouns.

_____ jacket   _____ book   _____ goat

_____ egg   _____ scarf   _____ igloo

_____ apple   _____ cake   _____ oven

_____ octopus   _____ animal   _____ gate

Q2 Now add **a** or **an** in front of these adjectives.

_____ young…   _____ interesting…   _____ smelly…   _____ amazing…

_____ sad…   _____ worried…   _____ open…   _____ cold…

Q3 Write four nouns from **Q1** and four adjectives from **Q2** into four different sentences.

_____

_____

_____

_____

Look around your kitchen. Point to different objects and ask your child if it needs an 'a' or 'an'.
If your child grasps this quickly you could introduce the exceptions to the rule: 'an' is also used
before a silent 'h' and 'a' is used with 'u' or 'eu' when the sound is 'y' (as in 'yes').

Speech marks

Q1 Write in the speech marks what is said in the speech bubbles.

It is time to leave.

"_____,"said Abby.

Do we have to?

"_____?"said Dom.

Yes, or we will be late.

"_____,"said Abby.

OK, I'm coming.

"_____,"said Dom.

Q2 Abby and Dom then go home and see their Mum.
Finish the conversation between Abby, Dom and their Mum.
What do you think Dom says next?

"_____," said Dom.

"_____," said Mum.

"_____," said Abby.

"_____," said Dom.

Prepositions 1

Prepositions compare the position of one thing to another.

The cat slept **in** the box.

Q1 Circle the preposition in each sentence.

The muddy dog jumped in the puddle.

Kylie sat beside her brother.

The horse jumped over the fence.

The walkers climbed up the hill.

Q2 Add a preposition to each of the sentences.

The old man walked _____ the bridge.

Garry swam _____ the icy pool.

Meena climbed _____ the tree.

Toby jumped _____ the wall.

Q3 Write your own sentences using the prepositions.

inside _____

behind _____

above _____

into _____

With your child look for the word 'position' in the word 'preposition'. Link it with the definition of a preposition (i.e. 'prepositions' compare the 'position' of one thing to another).

Paragraphs

Paragraphs are groups of **sentences** about a similar topic.
Paragraphs make it easier to read longer pieces of writing.
When a new **paragraph** is started the first line is usually indented.

  The children rushed home after school. They wanted to change
as quickly as possible for the party...

The Kelly family arrived at Blunsdon Caravan Park at 3.00pm. This gave them enough time to set up their caravan, unpack and have fun in the pool before tea. The next day they decided to explore the local area. First they headed to the shops to buy some food but then they went for a long walk along a coastal path, arriving at a beautiful beach.

Q1 Copy this short passage. Split it into two paragraphs.
Remember to indent the beginning of each paragraph.

Q2 Continue the passage, adding two more paragraphs describing what the Kelly family did that evening and then the next day.

_____

_____

_____

_____

_____

_____

_____

Paragraphs can be a tricky concept for children to pick up. The best way to reinforce paragraphs is to look at them in your child's own reading books or in a book you are reading to your child. Highlight why a new paragraph has been introduced each time.

Commas 1

Commas are used to separate items in a list.

My garden is home to a shy rabbit, a small mouse,
a sneaky fox and a friendly badger.

Q1 Write these lists into sentences.

> book   toothbrush   pyjamas   teddy   flannel

_____

> flute   clarinet   oboe   trumpet   violin

_____

Q2 Add the missing commas to these sentences.

Carl packed his football boots towel mouth guard and shorts ready for the match.

Mum bought crisps sweets biscuits and fruit for the party.

Aimee loved feeding the bouncing lambs cute baby rabbits pink piglets and
long-legged foal.

Q3 Write three of your own sentences that include lists.
The subjects in the box will give you some ideas.

> football   school   food   friends   holidays   colours

_____

_____

_____

This topic looks at commas in a list. Remind your child that a comma is not needed before the word
'and' which comes before the final word in the list.

Pronouns 1

Pronouns are used instead of **nouns**.
Pronouns avoid repeating **nouns** in **sentences**.

Tim walked the dog before *Tim* went to meet *Tim's* friends.
Tim walked the dog before **he** went to meet **his** friends.

Q1 Use the pronouns in the box to complete the sentences.

I   it   we   you   them

Jay said _____ was his book.

The teacher asked _____ if their boots were clean.

_____ love to eat hot chips.

Can _____ go to the Ice Show?

Did _____ see who made that mess?

Q2 Underline the pronouns in the sentences.

They loved performing and the parents watched them with pride.

"That is hot," she said.

It frightened me.

He came to visit us but we were out.

Q3 Copy the sentence, replacing the underlined words with a pronoun.

Laila looked forward to seeing the boy each weekend.

_____

Ask your child to list as many pronouns as they can.

16

Connectives

Two **sentences** can be joined when a word is added between them. The *joining word* is called a **connective**.

Tom tripped on the kerb. He didn't hurt himself.
Tom tripped on the kerb **but** he didn't hurt himself.

Connectives are sometimes called **conjunctions**.

Q1 The words in the box can all be connectives.
Copy and join each pair of sentences using a different connective.

| however | or | so | as | because | but | yet | and | when |

Darren tried to call Gareth. His phone had no service.

_____

Sunita climbed to the top of a tree. She wasn't scared at all.

_____

John was very hungry. He hadn't had any breakfast.

_____

Q2 Complete these sentences.

The radio played Kate's favourite song **but** _____

_____

Alex will finish his homework **when** _____

_____

Q3 Write your own sentence using this connective.

so _____

Verbs (to be)

The verb **to be** is very common.
It can either be used on its own *or* used to help another **verb**.

The horse **is** black.   The horse **is** *eating*.

Present tense: is   are
Past tense: was   were

Q1 Add the correct form of the verb **to be** to the sentences.

The lions _____ chasing the buffalo.   [is *or* are?]

Jamie _____ not feeling very well.   [is *or* are?]

Janine _____ a great gymnast.   [was *or* were?]

The children _____ late for school.   [was *or* were?]

Q2 Write sentences of your own using the verb **to be**, as listed below.

is   _____

was   _____

are   _____

were   _____

Q3 The noun form has to match the verb form.
Fill the gap in the sentences with the correct noun form.

The _____ *were* delicious.   [sweet *or* sweets?]

The _____ *is* asleep.   [baby *or* babies?]

The _____ *was* jumping around.   [lamb *or* lambs?]

With your child look for examples of the verb 'to be' in their reading book. Is the 'to be' verb used on its own or is it helping another verb (e.g. is jumping)?

Phrases

Phrases are short groups of words.
Phrases don't make sense on their own.
Phrases usually don't have a verb.

The ball was kicked **over the hedge**.

over the hedge is a phrase.

Q1 Which of the following are phrases? Write the phrases below.

The girls chatted.

in the kitchen   It began to rain.

along the beach   He had to wait.   through the keyhole

_____

_____

_____

Q2 Complete these sentences with a phrase.

The friends played with the ball _____

Dad drove carefully _____

Q3 Write the phrases into your own sentences.

through the village

_____

on the phone

_____

Ensure that your child spends time looking at the difference between a sentence and a phrase. Later they will become aware of the different types of phrases (adjectival, adverbial and noun phrases) but for now it is important they recognise what a phrase is.

Adjectives 2

Adjectives are describing words.
They tell us more about nouns.

The dog slept soundly.
The **exhausted**, **muddy** dog slept soundly.

Adjectives make writing more interesting.

Q1 Look at the picture.
Write adjectives to describe
the nouns.

greenhouse _____

boy _____

ball _____

Q2 Rewrite these sentences adding at least two adjectives to make them more interesting.

The leaves fell off the tree.

_____

My sister is annoying.

_____

My bike was bought on ebay.

_____

The camel spat in my face.

_____

Show your child an object they might not recognise. Encourage them to write as many different adjectives about it as they can.

Prepositions 2

Prepositions compare the position of one thing to another.

The cat walked **on** the table.

Q1 List the prepositions found in this passage.

Jess searched in the wardrobe and under the bed. She hunted inside the cupboards, looking among the clothes. She desperately wanted to find her birthday present. She was sure her mum had hidden it somewhere in her bedroom!

_____   _____   _____

_____   _____

Q2 Finish the sentences with a preposition and ending.

Daniel jumped _____

Hannah slept _____

The teacher looked _____

The snow lay _____

Q3 Write your own sentences using the prepositions.

among _____

beyond _____

within _____

The following words are all prepositions: towards, upon, beyond, by, near, within, past, off, inside, into, behind, above, about, on, across, against, at, among, beside. Ask your child to make a list of all the prepositions they can.

Adverbs

Adverbs tell us more about **verbs**.
They give a **verb** more meaning.

Alan **excitedly** opened his presents.

Adverbs tell us how, when or where something happens or is done.

Q1 Look carefully at the sentences. Circle the adverb in each one.

The mum gently laid down her baby.

Kylie sang beautifully.

Always check for cars carefully.

We quickly ran for the bus.

Q2 Use each of these adverbs in your own sentences.

sensibly _____

angrily _____

quietly _____

fiercely _____

Q3 Complete the table with adverbs that can be used with these verbs.

walk	draw	argue	eat

This topic deals with adverbs of manner, however there are two other types. These are adverbs of time (when actions take place) and adverbs of place (where actions take place).

Parts of speech

Parts of speech are the names of types of words.

Nouns, verbs, adjectives, prepositions, pronouns, adverbs and connectives are all parts of speech.

Q1 Write which part of speech each underlined word is.

Jenny <u>happily</u> <u>played</u> <u>on</u> the <u>fallen</u> tree <u>when</u> <u>she</u> got home from <u>school</u>.

Q2 Write your own sentences. Include and underline the listed parts of speech.

noun   adjective   pronoun

_____

verb   adverb   connective

_____

noun   adverb   preposition

_____

verb   preposition   pronoun

_____

This topic revises the parts of speech your child has learnt so far. Remind your child of the previous topics, running through any aspects they are confused about.

Pronouns 2

Pronouns are used instead of **nouns**.
Pronouns avoid repeating nouns in **sentences**.

> Veejay's dad bought *Veejay* a new puppy.
> Veejay's dad bought **him** a new puppy.

Pronouns can be singular or plural.

Q1 Circle the pronouns.

him   it   when   **behind**   we   where   **them**   return   on   **you**

Q2 Complete the table with the words from the box.

> her   us   they   he   she   we

Singular pronouns	Plural pronouns

Q3 Copy the sentences, replacing the <u>underlined</u> words with pronouns so it makes sense.

Tom jumped in a puddle so <u>Tom</u> could splash his brother.

_____

Finn and Ben are twins and <u>Finn and Ben</u> are often mixed up.

_____

Lucy has a puppy and <u>Lucy</u> enjoys playing with <u>her puppy</u>.

_____

Direct speech

Speech marks or **inverted commas** (" ...") show the exact words someone has spoken. This is called **direct speech**.

"The film starts in ten minutes," said Sonia.

What the person says is written inside the **speech marks**.

Q1 Copy the sentences. Add the missing speech marks.

I wish this lesson would finish, said Tuhil.

_____

Why? asked Mark.

_____

I am starving and want my lunch, answered Tuhil.

_____

Didn't you have a snack earlier? said Mark.

_____

Q2 Write a conversation you have recently had.
Remember to use speech marks.

_____ , said _____ .

_____ , said _____ .

_____ , said _____ .

_____ , said _____ .

_____ , said _____ .

Comparative and superlative adjectives

Adjectives are describing words.

A **comparative adjective** compares two **nouns**. Many **comparative adjectives** end in **er**.

A **superlative adjective** compares three or more nouns. Many **superlative adjectives** end in **est**.

big

bigger

biggest

Q1 Complete the sentences with words from the box.

> long   longer   longest   hot   hotter   hottest

My drink is _____, Mum's is _____

but Dad's is the _____.

Deena's daisy chain is _____, Becky's is

_____ but Heidi's is the _____.

Q2 Complete the table. **Remember** to check your spellings.

Adjective	Comparative	Superlative
small		
		wettest
	softer	
large		
		prettiest

Q3 Write these adjectives into a sentence.   **busy   busier   busiest**

_____

Apostrophes

An **apostrophe** can show when someone owns something.

One owner	= noun + **'s**	Kate**'s**
More than one owner	= noun + **'s**	children**'s**
More than one owner	= **but** noun ending in s + **'**	girls**'**

Q1 These are all singular nouns. Copy the phrase and add the missing apostrophe.

the builders hat

_____

the horses saddle

_____

the nurses thermometer

_____

the climbers rope

_____

Q2 These are all plural nouns. Copy the phrase and add the missing apostrophe.

the animals food

_____

the childrens sweets

_____

the flowers stems

_____

the policemens helmets

_____

Q3 Write each phrase into a sentence. **Remember** to add the missing apostrophe.

Bens books

_____

pigs piglets

_____

This topic covers apostrophes used for possession. This is a very difficult topic for children to grasp. Work through the rules found on this page with your child. Discourage your child from adding apostrophes anywhere, only when they know they are needed.

Commas 2

Commas are used to *separate items in a list.*
Commas can also be used to *show where there is a slight pause.*
This helps a reader understand what they are reading.

In a cavern, deep under the ocean, lived a
sea monster.

Q1 Add the missing commas to these sentences.

Gita the youngest in the choir sang beautifully.

The cat wet and shivering tried to get home out of the rain.

The heavy snow fell throughout the night leaving roads icy and dangerous.

Tanya rushed to the station arriving just as the train was about to leave.

Q2 Look at these sentences. How many commas are missing in each one?

The policeman brave and courageous caught the burglar.

Grass grows quickly through summer slowing during the winter months.

Najib who came first in the chess competition was delighted.

Jane who fell off the climbing frame was comforted by Mrs Hill.

Q3 Write the sentences in **Q2**. Include the missing commas.

_____

_____

_____

_____

Main clauses

A **main clause** is a group of words that is the main part of a **sentence** and could be a **sentence** by itself.

> **Our sheep** love to **eat** apples, though too many can make them ill.

> A **main clause** (underlined) must contain a *subject* (main thing or person) and *a verb*.

Q1 List the subject and verb in each of the underlined main clauses.

The teacher tidied the classroom before he went home.

_____   _____

The dog chased after the ball which my grandad had given her.

_____   _____

A lion pounced on its prey and ate it greedily.

_____   _____

Q2 Write these subjects and verbs into a main clause.

> deer   to eat

_____

> sister   to annoy

_____

Q3 Underline the main clause in these sentences.

The dentist pulled out one of my teeth which really hurt!

I dropped my book in a puddle on the way home from school.

Ensure your child knows the difference between phrases (covered on p. 19) and the clauses covered in this topic. Phrases are usually short and don't have a verb, clauses contain verbs and they can be a sentence in their own right.

How am I doing?

The next two pages revise many grammar and punctuation subjects covered in this book.

If you get stuck, look back at earlier topics.

Q1 Copy the sentences.
Add the missing **speech marks**.

Are we nearly there yet? asked Tuhil.

_____

It is freezing outside, said Jake.

_____

I feel very tired tonight, yawned Meg.

_____

Q2 Add **a** or **an** in front of the nouns.

____ dog   ____ elephant   ____ bucket

____ cup   ____ icebox   ____ monk

____ lock   ____ angel   ____ towel

____ explorer   ____ icicle   ____ wagon

Q3 Add an **adverb** to each of the sentences.

The children played _____.

The trees blew _____ in the wind.

Fiona slept _____ despite the storm.

I ran _____ to get help.

Q4 Add the missing punctuation.

Watch out the wall might collapse

Where are we going to eat

Go and tidy your room

Q5 Complete the table with words from the sentence.

The sheep raced into the lush field and they quickly started to eat the grass.

noun	verb	adjective	preposition	pronoun	connective

Q6 Copy the phrase and add the missing apostrophe.

the lions cub _____

the childrens parents _____

the teachers car park _____

Q7 Complete the table.

singular	plural
family	
	stories
pony	
	cities

When a noun ends in a consonant + **y**, the **y** is changed to an **i** before **es** is added.

Q8 Write the comparative and superlative adjectives for each of the adjectives.

old _____ _____

red _____ _____

Go back to the topics that your child still finds tricky.

31

Answers

Sentences
Page 4
1. We lay on the beach reading our books.
   The sea was cold but we had fun.
   Our sandwiches had sand in them.
2. Watch out, that dog looks cross!
   Come towards me slowly.
   Whose dog is it?
   The dog wandered off towards the pond.
3. Child's own sentences ending in a full stop, question mark and exclamation mark.

Nouns
Page 5
1. Chosen nouns added to the end of given sentences.
2. The <u>horse</u> cantered towards the <u>hedge</u>.
   On <u>Friday</u> we are going to <u>Cheltenham</u> to visit <u>Uncle Matt</u>.
   The <u>dentist</u> pulled out my wobbly <u>tooth</u>.
3. September
   London
   The Queen
   Christmas
   e.g. David Beckham

Verbs
Page 6
1. Dan licks his ice cream quickly.
   Dad mows the lawn every Saturday.
   Sarah bought a newspaper at lunchtime.
   The swing broke when Jay sat on it.
2.

Present tense verbs	Past tense verbs
shouts	wrote
skips	danced
laughs	drank
sleeps	painted

3. Two of child's own sentences written in the past tense.

Adjectives 1
Page 7
1. The Walton family walked in the (cold) wind.
   The toddler slipped on the (wet) mud.
   The (three) children ran to the park.
   The (grumpy) cat scratched Tom's hand.
2. Adjectives added to the gaps in sentences.
3. Each of the listed adjectives written into child's own sentences.

Questions
Page 8
1. Child's three questions written for a named adult.
2. e.g. Are you going to be warm enough?
   e.g. Where are we going for tea?
   e.g. Will you buy some milk?
   e.g. What time are you arriving?

Exclamations
Page 9
1.

Pain!	Surprise!	An order!
That hurt!	I don't believe it!	Don't touch!
Help, I can't move my foot!	Watch out!	Quick, get over here!
Ouch, please don't!	Wow, look at that!	Stop, right now!

2. Child's own examples of exclamations.

Singular and plural
Page 10
1.

Singular	Plural
class	classes
fox	foxes
dish	dishes
glass	glasses
lunch	lunches
bush	bushes

2. The <u>dresses</u> looked beautiful on the <u>bridesmaids</u>.
   The <u>apples</u> and <u>peaches</u> tasted delicious.
   The farmer checked his <u>fields</u> before letting in the <u>cows</u>.
   Mrs Damage dropped the tray of <u>dishes</u> and <u>glasses</u>.
3. dress, bridesmaid, apple, peach, field, cow, dish, glass

Articles (a and an)
Page 11
1. a jacket, a book, a goat, an egg, a scarf, an igloo, an apple, a cake, an oven, an octopus, an animal, a gate
2. a young…, an interesting…, a smelly…, an amazing…, a sad…, a worried…, an open…, a cold…
3. Four sentences using nouns from Q1 and adjectives from Q2.

Speech marks
Page 12
1. "It is time to leave," said Abby.
   "Do we have to?" said Dom.
   "Yes, or we will be late," said Abby.
   "Ok, I'm coming," said Dom.
2. The child continues the conversation between Abby, Dom and Mum.

Prepositions 1
Page 13
1. The muddy dog jumped (in) the puddle.
   Kylie sat (beside) her brother.
   The horse jumped (over) the fence.
   The walkers climbed (up) the hill.
2. e.g. The old man walked *across* the bridge.
   e.g. Garry swam *in* the icy pool.
   e.g. Meena climbed *up* the tree.
   e.g. Toby jumped *over* the wall.
3. The child's own sentences using the given prepositions.

Paragraphs
Page 14
1. The Kelly family arrived at Blunsdon Caravan Park at 3.00pm. This gave them enough time to set up their caravan, unpack and have fun in the pool before tea.
   The next day they decided to explore the local area. First they headed to the shops to buy some food but then they went for a long walk along a coastal path, arriving at a beautiful beach.
2. Story continued for a further two paragraphs.

Commas 1
Page 15
1. The child's own sentences using the given lists of words.
2. Carl packed his football boots, towel, mouth guard and shorts ready for the match.
   Mum bought crisps, sweets, biscuits and fruit for the party.
   Aimee loved feeding the bouncing lambs, cute baby rabbits, pink piglets and long-legged foal.
3. Three of child's own sentences that include lists.

Pronouns 1
Page 16
1. Jay said it was his book.
   The teacher asked them if their boots were clean.
   I/We love to eat hot chips.
   Can we/I go to the Ice Show?
   Did you see who made that mess?